"The world is
a wedding"
waiting to happen
to you.

Love from David
May 20, 1995

Pick Up the House

ANSELM HOLLO

PICK UP THE HOUSE

NEW & SELECTED POEMS

COFFEE HOUSE PRESS   MINNEAPOLIS   1986

Drawings and back-cover photo by Jane Dalrymple-Hollo.

Thanks to the originators of the following publications, in which some of these works have appeared, many of them in earlier versions:

Baltimore Sun Sunday Magazine, Carolina Quarterly, City Paper (Baltimore), The Coherences (Trigram Press), Cream City Review, Exquisite Corpse, Faces & Forms (Ambit), Heavy Jars (Toothpaste Press), Ink, Open 24 Hours, Quarry West, Sagetrieb, St. Mark's Poetry Newsletter, Smithereens Sampler.

The publishers wish to thank the National Endowment for the Arts, a federal agency, for a Small Press Assistance Grant that aided in the production of this book.

Coffee House Press books are distributed to the trade by CONSORTIUM, 213 East Fourth Street, St. Paul, MN 55101.

Library of Congress Cataloging-in-Publication Data

Hollo, Anselm.

    Pick up the house.
    I. Title.
PR6015.0415P5   1986   821'.914   86-4143
ISBN 0-918273-18-8

Contents

When having something to do
but not yet being at it
because I'm alone, because of you
I lay down the book, & pick up the house

& move it around until it is
where it is what it is I am doing
that is the something I had to do
because I'm no longer alone, because of you.

— Ted Berrigan, *Coda: Song*

For Jane,
"pigga ögon"

The Sixties & Thereabouts, 1959–1965

"He repented
on his deathbed
seeing the great evil
he and his men had done"

      The false consolations of
      "history"
              as taught to children

      some of them
      destined to march
      two by two follow your leader
          (who did not die
          in a bed)
      your leader
            to a truck in a field

         littered
         with skulls & shoes
         later

*

The photograph, remembered

Polish boy, six or seven

Cloth cap on his head
         still on scrawny neck

      –BURN
      two holes
      in this page:

           his eyes

Evensong 1965

After a good day's work,
the military scientist
sits listening to his hi-fi set
but does not realize that his depraved
motorcyclist son
has substituted Ray Charles for Maria Callas.
The military scientist has protruding ears
all clogged up with radioactive dust
and his president's speeches. He sits there
smiling, a little cobalt angel
in his open-plan house, in full view
of millions of stars and the desert,
a good day's work.

The rain
heavier on our bodies the year
October: an eye and a mouth: our bodies
moved through the frightening dark of smiles
on faces unseen. What thoughts in their power beds
sleeping   waving   coming up for air
Who are they who force us to walk
the streets past houses shaking with steam
and fear? Toward each other my love to walk to walk.
Will they stop us, who are They? Bodies
rolling, groaning...To wake, not to wake
to morning decisions and twitching eyelids, the eyes
nails of lead in their brains
& heavy, our feet in their sleep, what gestures,
distances, who walks here, on our legs?

*

In his brain
blockaded by sleep
a child sits in the one small well-lit room.
It is drawing a picture: an island, an eye
staring, out of the blue ocean face,
and he says, "Cuba," in his sleep: "I never went there."

The child turns, smiles. It is thinking
of Christmas.

The dreamer sees a tin-plate fire engine
in the child's mouth – going
in.

...watched you
& you were turning, turning
from me, & back to me, you were light & dark
both, in ever-shifting proportion
as were the questions that whirled in my head

– question answered by question, your voice & mine
following, leading, leading us where? where
were we going, where could we go, if we would, when
we would, and what were the reasons given,
the best way to get there, through rooms & streets,
the blueing desert, encased in time

watched you, trying to read your face

wandered in light halls, dark caves, held by the wind
piercing us beyond pleasure or pain: that constant spear

watched us, resting, bodies stretched out on a shield
in a place with many old gods on the walls: did they
whisper & hum, back through their millions of lives,
through time? I could not hear them, only your breath,

only the songs of your body, your face: an intricate
chant, an enchantment, clear in all its relations

high, high on it, in the place we had reached
I was open to you, your music, not watching but seeing
you – light
              in the dark
                        that shines beyond walls or time

Night Wind Pieces

before & after, thus, for Carl Rakosi

The wind, let loose in the dark:
the lights of the city, moving –

the city is a great dragon, it is a procession,
it is on the move:

but the curtains are drawn, the music's unheard –
see: men and women, preparing themselves

for the long journey
across a room

*

A paddy wagon, with a man's face
in the steel-mesh window –
a green van, and a pig's snout
looking out:
contemplating their destinations,
a fuzzy head
atop my peacoat

*

Another night, another window:
she has been brushing her hair
fully an hour

The other, behind his dark wishing window,
eyes spanning the width of uncaring shoulders

Having wiped
his shriveling eyes off the sill
she draws the curtains

The light, round the edges: an eclipse

Friend Fiends

One by one, caught in their secret gardens:
sun in his head, leaning against a Notting Hill
lamppost, oh hate to see it go down that dark cell drain
hiding it in the TV set neighbors told them
"he never turned it on" or Camden Town basement
sounds laughter and smoke, *eheu fugaces* oh evil fruit
pushing a pound or two of it through Golder's Green
a baby carriage, two babies on top, surprised by bobbies
groping their little damp bottoms, oh drug fiends.
Or, on the way home on the Circle Line, six packets
of good Ghanaian fell out of his umbrella, ay-ay-ay

To say good morning blues how do you do
something is sneaking round the corner
not about the weather
myself I'm feeling pretty bad
not about the climate
you are adorable
but of certain limitations
myself I'll go to Spain one of these days
but of no importance
all of you are wonderful people
and to say it is a great pleasure indeed
with a lilt

Parting

after Hugo Ball

Don't go
      is what I want you to tell me

The rainless south wind
will make me long for you

Tell me
      these are beautiful days
to have you here   to look at your mouth
and to listen
            Don't go

Tell me life pleases you

Tell my voice to go on and on

Tell me you will be happy and of good cheer
even when I am gone

Tell me I'm stupid

            a child   or feathers & a small brain
                        held in your hand

Tell me I know
            my way back to you
even at night
in the rain that hides the stars

Dream Rain Dance

for Anne Sher

Listen, to rain swishing down –
good empty sound
    after all the voices
but only then: a moment's
      unloneliness. Listened
  to a friend's voice, remembering
how she told me her dream, months ago.
It was about driving along flat country
   straight road toward a herd
    of what seemed to be
   elephants
   only their shape
      was pyramids,
   no visible eyes or mouths
   no apertures at all:
yet, all at once, she knew
   they moved in a dance, of three
    figures only –
 sex food companionship

She was driving toward them, but not getting
any closer. She would never
reach them. Felt
   regret, but also a sense of
    exhilaration:
   while driving, she found
 she could figure all the possible
   permutations: "I give you A (food),
you give me B (sex), he she it withhold C
    (companionship)," etc., etc.

Imagine! she said, about a hundred of them
– and I knew it all, all they could ever
   and would ever
    do…

just like that, in my head, and me!
                 who has trouble with sums...

It seemed
a sad dream, at the time. Now
it's quite a bit funnier, too:

"When the sky gets cloudy & it look like rain,

that's a sure sign the weather's gonna change"

Leadbelly's sound on the record
we sat nodding to
           in one night's companionship.

         On record, yes,
there have been those who could give it all
– A, B, C. Rare voices
         of little mathematical interest.

             Your eyes
         in the dark, and shimmering
         hair, a cloud
            come to rest for a
         moment's
                 unloneliness.

         My arms were aching
from holding on so long to my heroic balloon.

It was good to see you that close, to hear your voice
         from no distance at all, in July 1966

         and to be your "beatnik Walter de la Mare"

         in the pantheon we share

         with Al Alvarez, a totally great guy.

One day he was singing
his way through the fields when he saw
a cow stop grazing to listen

He was enchanted
but when he looked closer
realized that she was simply peeing

It was a good story   Brancusi

In the bathroom my friend had a pinup
his "Endless Pillar"

I stood there   peeing & looking
listening   to the music my peeing
& looking & listening made

on my independent sound system

How Sad Is the Mechanical Moose!

in the Kalevala or otherwise

anguish
your lot when the heart
                    beats like a metronome
            bowels
                    move with the whir
            & clank of the assembly line
& your eyes
                    blur nothing, all
                            is seen in meaningless detail
            anguish
shines in his eyes at night
                    he believes he is standing still
            in suffering contemplation
yet his legs move, the oils flow
    into the joints & bearings the durable synthetic skin
creasing uncreasing on steel flanks

        twigs break, cones crackle, ground thunders

his ears ticking it all away on tape
            spool coiling snug in his belly

he hears & does not hear & stands still
in his programed mind an enormous silent effort
            to wrench one cog to slip & clench another –

        to generate a wail

    factory siren in a ghost town, or train
            become invisible immaterial pure sound, an error –

        desolate hoot

                quite predictive

From *Heavy Jars*, 1975–1977

After Novalis

The scribe is writing
indefatigably

casting now and again
only a sullen glance
at the children

scowling grimly
while handing the pages
to a noble
goddesslike woman

who stands
leaning
against an altar

upon which rests
a dark vessel with clear water

She dips the pages
into this water

& when upon drawing them forth
she sees that some of the writing
has held fast

she gives that page
back to the scribe

who then binds it
in a Great Book

but often seems peevish
when his efforts prove vain

& everything has been obliterated

Slowly
the eye scans the page

The heart
beats steadily

while the mind winces in
in infinitesimal
spasms of almost prenatal pleasure

Down in the street
it is divided
into three parts:
sidewalk, street proper,
sidewalk: large things
of equally inelastic matter
on either side

These, inhabited
by home-grown beings

several of whom are reading too

the karmic revelations
of so many
silly and lovable cells

conjoined in the bliss that feeds
them, and on them, too

Thus holding them

(now turn the page)

Awkward Spring
has spilled its
golden ink
all over the angels' bibs

& off
the swan's soft chest
white feathers fall
into the swamp

& so forth

& I thought I was

a big & perfectly sensible dog

walking the other dog

with some dignity

thinking not of Form 0412-dash-70144

but of a City

equal to my Desire

Landing in the Trees

outside the car
window bright clumps
of hibernating chumps

Pop of guns, light rain

Driving south
over the washed-out fens

Tired
of the single tricycle's squeak
It is time to land
safely, in the park

But the huge nest
we hoped to spot
is gone

into some cave outside our map

Huge wings snap

& incidents increase until
they cannot be ignored

In the pyramid
the children get bored

We pull the covers
higher
            things brighten

Moon slips through blue spruce

a million miles away, bright & loud, like frog

Helsinki, 1940

Exploding, shattering, burning

Big lights in the sky

& this was
Heaven's Gate?

No no it's just the front door
same old front door you know from the daytime
& we're just waiting for a lull in the action
to cross the yard, get down to the shelter
& meet the folks, all the other folks
from all the other apartments

& there was a young woman
at least ten years older
he thought very beautiful

Blankets & wooden beams & crackling radios & chatter

It was better than heaven, it was
being safe in the earth ground, surrounded by many

all of whom really felt like living

Big Dog

I bring you
this head,
full of breath-
takingly beautiful
images of yourself

& put it in
your lap.

Now I breathe
more quietly.

Now you pat me.

Now I sigh.

In a moment or two
I'll get up and
be a man again.

It Is Hot

The picture, it flies
off the wall like a bat

Up & down & around we go
on the convolute ladders of light

Wavering foci
in the great boogie-woogie of creation
insistent
beyond notions of size or reason

Continuously propelling
the mind's components
through a wind tunnel without walls

& with no particular purpose
other than the sensational:

A voice, both gracious & warm, in the other room

Another, from
another universe

crying
        for its mate in the yard

            (& what did you just say?)

Botanica

Coleus
& corn plant
on the window ledge

New friends
under the sun

Past them, I see the neighbors'
purple rosebush
in gigantic bloom

In the tinkle of time
we shall be
released
back into
the realm of
photosynthesis

& that's a thought,
a mandragoric thought

Sweet Monster Babe

tall as trees
in windy sunlight

When I was born,
I yelled and screamed

Yesterday's news, if mythic

Both ends, it is tough

But here in the middle
the mind waves

in tune with the wild
heads of camomile
archangels

A Toke for Li Po

Born in Pa-Hsi province
of Szechwan

Lived *muchos años*
at the court of the emperor

Ming Huang but was banished
as a result of falling
in disfavor? with the empress
Kao Li-Shih, & wandered about China thereafter

only occasionally attached to a patron
leading a "dissolute" life, addicted? to drink
writing the poems about the joys of that life

notably wine & women & all the rest
& agitation of the sensational universe

Came to his death by falling
out of a boat & drowning
in an attempt to have intimate intercourse
with the moon
in the water

One of those of
whom it is said,

"He took the charge well"

Pick Up The House, 1981–1985

In the Mission

for Robert Creeley

God

His
followers
started the place but

God
is not what you think
in the Mission

*

As the song
goes, "The good
times, the bad
times"

God knows
back there,
in his snug chair
on the favorite floor

of his perishing tower
wistful,
sniffing
a flower:

"Reminds me of
all of them"

*

Be a hundred and ten.
Go to sleep.

38　　Say,
"*Au revoir.*"

*

She used to be angry,
but now she is sleeping:

"Oh let me dwell in
comfortable-looking
hole in your facial cheek"

*

See See

Five short yellow
dafs – narcissi –
whatever they are,

flowers of spring
tra-la, suddenly
in this lone kitchen sing

a scent sweet, it says,
"Si, si"

•　•　•

Most of life not
that way,
yet one remembers

when it has been, been seen
and heard and felt, and smelled
that way.

*

Life is complicated
Drains are roaring
Percy B. Shelley
was fond of soaring

In walks a minimalist
He says, "That's boring"
He needs to be kissed
by someone complicated

Another sweet
big head
to remain entertained
and a bit more alive than dead

*

High Cloud

Populous raft of confusion
drifting across the sky
while fur turns gray

*

Rimas

I haven't lost my mind, you know,
although I think, believe, I've found
a woman, most intelligent, most kind,
with whom I then proceed to fight
on what I thought was an auspicious night –
about what, neither of us know.

There is the rain, there is the snow,
the dew, the fog, the mist, the glow,

the atmosphere containing us
and the necessity to catch the bus.
Hers. Mine. Possessive forms of action
giving one little or no traction.

So let it slide, and let's abide and sigh
as dawn is drawing nigh and fires are lit again
throughout the camps of busyness and gain.

I love her eyes: love them when they look at me,
her mouth when it moves, even when not speaking.

*

In the summer, he said, I write short

*

Now that people are wearing hats again,
one can tell them "Go shit in your hat" again

*

Make her laugh: the world
seems like it's staying

*

"They only made one of these.
Do you deserve it?"

*

Who's here?

Two powerful Democrats
Many United Beef Workers
Some Undecided Youths

"Just white poet trash"
    – The Decisive Instrumentality

*

A High Note

leaves one at a loss
for an appropriate quote

and so, remembering, one says, "Hello,"
and says, into dark air, "You're very nice,"

rolls over, hugs
oneself, and wants you back

*

Back in New York

"My sister, life" – last time I saw her
I begged her not to be as literal as me;
old flames, old blames – none there
that precious funky afternoon: yes,

some lives work: somewhere in here's
this romantic boy, writes letters in his head
and in his heart – which are the faces
he makes, in there, inside himself.

And once in a while he jumps up on the shelf
and sits there: looking at you: eyes all one color.

*

You're not gonna sleep
anyway
You're just gonna lay
around and curse

So why not stay up, brother,
and think about everything

And I mean *everything*

*

Her face, absolutely
two sides

and sometimes, in motion,
unearthly harmonious

*

"To bed, to bed,
as Lady Macbeth said"

There was a time
one thought that was funny

An amusing
rhyme

*

Ferocious sociopath
rubs ace of hearts   .
against his crotch, for luck

Un *poco* buzzed, observing water's descent
upon phenomena, Thursday, also César
Vallejo's "bad day"

*

Clarification

Not
buying
you:

just
buying
you

a
drink

*

A Kind of a Vow

Make me
a pillow
and I'll
sleep on it
as long as it
takes me

*

Proofreading Discovery

"inextricably
interwoven"

became

44   "methodically
      intentional"

      *

      Shiva
      takes it
      apart and
      down,

      puts it
      together
      again
      in the ground –

      ("Aahh-yess, Shee-vah take it apart 'n'…")

      *

      Not going to read
      any of these
      to anyone
      over the phone
      tonight.

      Tonight is the night
      anyone's under the covers
      with their lovers
      present or not,
      present or not.

                          August 1981–August 1982
                          San Francisco

Mission Aubade

for Tinker Greene

Ambulance howls into receiving bay
Some birds start singing
Folks on the block are getting up
Some are still awake   still alive too

Long Ways

Come a long way,
speak of it now and again:
that is our work.

Twenty-four years ago honeymooned on the Isle
    of Jersey, our son on his way.
Low tide, we walked out to the castle,
warm, apprehensive, expectant, bored.
Slept and woke in the sweet and salt;
sea and light is what I remember.
Dreamt himself into being inside you,
now he has lived the years we had then:
a man, mind, heart, a peaceable builder
    of a future beyond ours.

Go a long way,
travel the seas in darkness and light,
speak of it now and then.

May it always ride in and out again
as in all the stories we love to hear:

horses
              strutting,
ships
          sliding into the harbor –
Lindy
          coming in to land,
Ted rolling out of bed –

greens
          turning to the light,
hands
       insistent in the night;

two people
                  playing accurate guitars
on this century's
                  twilight TV

Know the various abuses of the locution,
know all the shit one may have to eat in the afterhaze:
yet if you cannot say to another you, "I love you,"
how can you ever say anything anymore anywhere
        in this world?

How It Works

In the suburbs it's quite expensive
to hire an assassin – to get
the witness permanently removed.

In the projects it's quite a bit cheaper.

And elsewhere in not so civilized parts
it's absolutely a bargain.

And that's pretty much how it works.

50   *Valid*

Having a *pasaporte,* how much more *valid*
I am than brother Jésus or Pedro
trying to swim the river,
tackle the spiral barbed wire!

"The culture of a people
is an ensemble of texts
which the Anthropologist
strains to read"

over the shoulders of those to whom they properly belong

*

"The essay, whether of thirty pages
or three hundred, has seemed
the natural genre in which to present
cultural interpretations"

and the theories sustaining your jobs   you jokers

52   Some

Some thing falls
to some floor.

Someone remembers,
makes much of it.

The other one says,
I had no idea.

*

After the telephone
he sat a while trembling
the way dogs do when nervous
when they've perceived something
much larger than their brains

Hot sunny Baltimore day,
walking through the park,
holding her hand, touching her waist.
Checking out the zoo,
in and out the gates.
Sun sets.   Oh, Ted, we miss you,
whistling in the dark.

Cool
    April wind
blowing
      mulberry
petals, belated
         "snowflakes"
in the small
merciful
hours:

Came
    home,
walked into bathroom:

Aahh!   Colors!
Pretty shapes!

Your
    summer clothes
shedding their wrinkles
& mothball scent –

doing
    the things
I've been trying to do
ever since you told me

come in   come home

Wanting to wake you up at 3:00 A.M., knowing
you need rest more than my babble, I try
to calm down, sip tea, and breathe

my way through early morning hits and flashes

to a state approximating the seal that says

> *paper is too short*
> *for the endless affections*

or the one that says

> *it is a rare virtue*
> *to be able to muddle through*
> *once in a while*

or

> *how can I do without you,*
> *even for a day?*

Sixteenth, seventeenth China, not that far away,

which moves me next to you, Particular Woman,
half-despairing, sliding into my dreams, resisting

yet praying for your dear face next to mine

to be there

> to be there, at dawn

Match, struck, flares
                    in the dark

        Quark
flits through molecule and is gone

                        to traverse
                        yet another room

    *

Deities' noses twitch in their slumbers,

remember poetry and pinball:

love making no demand for love in return,

para siempre

In measured hand
we write the letter
full of rage

but then,
a little later,
feel our age

and say, Shit —
who's that do?
Some bodies

gun their cars
out of this street.
The sun

also rises. Nancy
and Sluggo
go to it.

Eros
totally involved love at first sight

Ludus
playful love – love as a game

Storge
love from a deep and lasting friendship

Pragma
love with a shopping list

Mania
unbalanced love involving extreme possessiveness

Agape
selfless love making no demand for love in return

Paradiso
all of the above in perfect perennially contradictory balance

YELL! CRY! SHOUT! WEEP! COMPLAIN!
Modes only too easy
in 1983
or any year this fast

in the fastest known century
of an upstart human universe
quite pitifully brief
while possibly unique

"I MEAN," says a lady
calling in on our private
all-night station,
"HOW CAN WE KNOW

THE CUCARACHAS WILL PRODUCE
ANOTHER HENRY JAMES"
or HARRY or FRANK
or JESSE for that matter

Ten trillion cells
exchanging coded info
every micro-instant in her head
(and yours and mine)

Yell shout weep cry complain
trying to hit that note
(can't sing) Oh timid timid time
of weaponry's highly

organized flowering
and wistful pleasure
in the Empire's cities
Crazed pain and its infliction

60   at outposts and bridgeheads
Broken bones hanks of
disenfranchised hair
by their roadsides

Oh timid timid time
in the Empire's last days
a headline: "RAT BITES FRIEND
EARLY ONE MORNING

LATE IN 1983"
and wistful pleasure
in sometimes cultivated
small spaces:

People
really
aren't
that large

and don't have to
devour
more than
their share

Who has a face sees
   the world,
but the world
   is not

to be borne —
   or only
when seen as
   another:

how did this
   come together? How
did I find you?
   So many turns

in the road,
   so few of them
possible!
   How not to spin out

in hairpin turns
   of disbelief...
The Sufi martyrs
   insisted:

"The world
   is a wedding."
Why not
   go with them,

in the face of
   present carnage,
centuries
   later.

Wandering
through the rooms,
touching things, gazing
in sad drunken nakedness

back in the wilderness,
he missed her, his guide

"no clothes on, and no use"

The body is frail,
even Odysseus',
given to him for a time (no
    mileage charge):
stretched muscles, pinched nerves,
    slipped disks, twisted joints,
        broken bones, ah yes –
There is
        a foot in the water,
alongside the boat

    and the toes
            feel pretty good

Amigo, we're buzzing along

A Round for the Trout Fisher

One: Back When There Was Bliss

"Ignorant bliss" –
 not ignorant of but ignoring
Death
 and rightly so,

as death is the cessation of knowing:
 hence what is worth keeping are
the living bodies: many of them

 exploding, imploding,
with anger, hunger,
 splattering
our lordly windshields.

 So stop the car – no, don't:
at any intersection in Brasília
 you'll be deconstructed

by a fountain of machetes,
 once you step out of
your shell.
 See the world, baby,

but stay in the cage is the password.
 So in our little quite comfy cages
we sit and quiver –

 one dances, one plays the flute.
Friends clack the cymbals,
 shake the tambourine. Once
in a while

 someone remembers
one of those old words:
 Equity.   Compassion.   Tenderness

and makes them
   iridesce
round the
   edges

Two: Two Scenarios, Or Simple Village Tunes

Well, things came up out of the ground
and GOT them.
Well, things fell down from the sky
and GOT them.
Well, the AIR got so bad, and the WATER,
it GOT them.

WELL, they just didn't
know what to look for:
there were too many things
they'd made, and didn't even
know, besides
the things

they hadn't made, and didn't know, either.

*

And then there were some who said, We don't think
we want to go, we think we want to stay
and look at this place a little longer

Not that it's going to improve by our doing so

Not that it's going to get worse

Just that we haven't really seen it yet

Just that we'd like to look at it a little longer

Primaries, conventions, elections –
spectacularly staged surrogates for old dreams
          of powwows by the campfire,
direct votes cast at the forum
          or Anglo-Saxon "thing"

Dreamy memories of just about postnomadic time
when the turnip was the new technology.
While knowing this was long ago, far away,
we'd still like to get next to the headperson
and deliver a speech, at least twice as long
          as anyone else's…

Even if telepathy were perfected –
and instant global communication –
where on earth would we find
statespersons, legislators, bureaucrats
able to withstand such an incredible onslaught
          of info? Would the result not be total
overload, fried circuits, the screaming meemies?

Yet each and every ant knows exactly what
          it has to be doing every second,
the whole shebang self-contained
and self-informing –

To paraphrase Blaise Pascal, I'd rather be
          a confused, blundering, warm-blooded
          hairy creature with language
to complain in, to praise with, no matter what,
than nature's prototype for the microchip.

Petit Chanson

One of those quiet moments
when things fall into shape
    and *be*: wind gently blowing
    residual raindrops
    against the window

daytime frazzle collapses
into sweet darkness

and the moment, while officially
3:00 A.M., is all the eternity
one will ever know

On the Occasion of a Poet's Death

The dedication and intensity of the dead
always were greater than ours.
No doubt it seemed that way to them too
as dusk was falling
on their last weary glimpse of a land
populated by twerps.

The disembodied glories of Hades await us.

Ascending mountain path
in good company: Ted Berrigan,
seen here the first time after his death –
Duncan McNaughton, still alive in the world I'm adream in,
many others
wearing sturdy United Beloved Nations overcoats, blue-black,
scarves, gloves, goodly shoes,
though there is one fellow with snazzy hat:
turned-up collar prevents me from seeing face
– Tinker Greene perhaps?
                              Well, anyway, here we go
in bright blue day,
mountain to our right,
sheer drop to miles away valleys
on our left – the path
beautifully paved, with pale gray, almost square chunks of stone,
the width of it
a person and a half

So we tread lightly and with care
while typically smoking this or that
(Doing this in waking life,
we'd be gasping, stumbling, quite easily gone)

Ted says, "Wouldn't you know it?"
apropos of what? There's also a strong wind,
and I am worrying about the emerald abyss
to my left
              yet confident we'll all make it
to wherever we're going that seemed
just around the corner
and now is, quite possibly, not merely
atop a mountain
                    but *inside* the mountain,
only to be reached by

an equal number of strides
                        down: on the inside: no shortcuts.

Hair, beards, coats, scarves flapping
in the emphatic wind,
glasses reflecting pale brightness,
we're walking, bullshitting along, just as in
real life. Hey, here's George Kimball III
with a bottle: Thanks, man: who or what "won"?

But careful now, one slip and we won't
feel so great anymore. On we go,
Ted our guide, friend, beloved raconteur...

Æons later, someone, Duncan I think, says, "You know,
we're going to give it back to them,"
and I think, Oh no, what's this? we're not just proceeding
to the most remote tavern of the universe?

And Ted says, "Yes, yes – we're going to
where the pounding of acceptance
meets the pummeling of negation – no, no"
(drags on Chesterfield King)
"which is utter benighted bullshit, of course"

Now there is sleet, even small hail in the wind,
and I remember the waking lifetime we strode
through blizzard in Minnesota, early Iowa morning rain,
and youthful demons on Lower East Side

And I think, There has to be a trick, to end this dream,
the way there are tricks to end a poem

                19–20 September 1984

Letter

Dear sister, where was it, where is it now,
we sat under a tree, and you were crying, and
I did not have the faintest as to why...
But I did. I knew it was because you were in love
with Col. Hercules Wilmot Scott, and there was no way
that anyone was going to understand that.

Hearing

for Jane

       great voices
of the great dead, next
to the great living you
(no TV): such thrills inside
led me here, to you. No
TV. Jonquils, soon dead, out
of season, in howling winds:
winter, cold moon. Your warm
belly, rubbed thrice for luck:
clear vision, smile in the morning –
"No war, please."

"Amazing Grace"

for Jane

Ted Berrigan's favorite hymn, more true
than anything I'd heard that year
but for your, my lady's, voice and being,

winging into my life, and so completely seeing
the holes Death had punched into my head –

freeing my heart to love again in ways
forgotten, known again:

the humble rage of love, its tears,
its spasms of joy, its fears, its sighs
and grand designs: amazing grace.

Put In a Quaver, Here and There

It is smooth, fairly
uniformly gray, and of a
topological conformation
not easily described by Euclid:
circa two inches wide,
one inch tall, and half an inch
in thickness.
          (I am indulging
in little twinges of nostalgia,
using those ancient
premetric
        and soon to be forgotten
measurements.)

        It is a rock
found on a beach
called Half Moon Bay
an easy hour's drive south of
    San Francisco,
picked out from among a great number
of fellow rocks and pebbles, ground and
washed ashore by the Pacific,
the most intimidating and also most beautiful
body of water
         on this planet. The reason
this artifact of an ocean
now sits on my desk,
facing St. Paul Street in Baltimore,
is its sculptural aspect. It has eyes,
nostrils, and a mouth,
all in unexpected places,
making it what the French call
un joli laid —
        a beautiful ugly one,

easily seen as the fossil skull of a small
Venusian, landed long ago
on some shore of earth. A miniature
henrymoore, it defies easy recognition,
arrests the eye, and makes one think of
other possible forms.

While knowing well that it's just a large pebble,
pointed out and handed to me by a friend
with whom I'd spent hours and days on that beach,
watching dogs chase pelican shadows across the shallows.

I also know that it is what the ancients knew as
    an "object of virtue" – irresistible –

        recently traveled to visit its shore of origin
        in another friend's purse, as a mascot,
        it did, indeed, bring her home safe and sound.

Daniel Spoerri, Swiss artist-philosopher,
friend and disciple of the great Duchamp,
made a book called *An Annotated Topography of Chance*.
This consists of a detailed description of each
and every object found on or around his studio table
on a given date, complete with the history
    of these objects' origins,
relationships to present circumstance, what have you:

Looking at my Venusian from Half Moon Beach,
now serving as humble paperweight, I am reminded
    of Spoerri's lovely undertaking,
and – what with a post-thunderstorm July sun
    shining into my window – encouraged to suggest
to all of you, dear friends, moments of contemplation
vis-à-vis accumulated objects of virtue
in your immediate vicinity: mute witnesses,
they could yet prove to be guides.

In the Voice of Jane to Her Mother

Caught myself
putting away four dresses
I've never worn,
folding them

into a suitcase
to wait for winter, again.
They were my mother's,
before my time –

when I
didn't know her.
She'd hoped
they would fit me:

they never did.
But their fabrics are fine,
indeed,
the stuff of dreams:

that a piece of cloth
be revived to new use,
that my mother
be my friend.

Late Night Dream Movies

for Chris Toll

1

The war beneath the seas
is quiet.
St. Paul Street, Baltimore, at 1:30 A.M.,
is not.
But I'd sure as hell rather be here
than in some sinister submarine.
I don't know – why
am I telling you this? Who *are* you?
Yelling, out there. Well, I'm yelling
in here too.

2

Heavyset, self-assured fellow
at marble-top café table
keeps pointing at peacoat
suspended from Martini Rossi parasol
and saying, "You mean you don't *have*
another coat?"
Shivering
in my underwear, I rage back:
"That's the *only* coat I have!"
Grab his lapels, haul off, and,
almost connecting
with his hateful Sidney Greenstreet smirk,
wake up to Jane's startled yet smiling face
and her saying, "You just punched me in the chest?"

3

Now we are in scenic Iowa City,
in a motel
with sliding glass doors fronting on Olympic-size
patio swimming pool: it must be some kind of
conference – here comes Jane, with hardly
any clothes on, followed by patently upset and
expostulating Father – she stops, turns, leans forward,
and tells him, "Why don't you just go suck on a
big fat cigar!" Crash, boom, Rachmaninoff. Next thing
I know, we're sitting at table among dinner debris,
Jane at far end, in some animation,
Dave Beaudoin, looking most proper, on my left,
Father across from us: we're having coffee,
brandy, it is quite warm,
but Papa has been weeping – his shoulders, even, are wet –
and after sympathetic murmurs, and a short pause,
he pulls out a somewhat musket-shaped clarinet from his pocket,
which turns out to be a cigar holder – affixes
big cigar to it, starts puffing – I say,
"But can you play it, too?" He says, "Sure," and gives us
a tune. I think this is quite certainly better
than last night's number, when I was climbing
the scaffolding of a giant roller coaster
in order to get back to my life, my words.

4

The castle, cut off by the tide: we're moving in on it
in these nifty inflatable two-person assault rafts, just
before dawn. Granular silver surrounds us. We're
on time, we'll be there right on time. The Great Electric
Eel is our impartial observer: we'll avoid bloodshed. We
owe it to him. Jane smiles at me through the spray: she is
the most beautiful human I've ever seen.
I squeeze her long fingers: "It'll be all right."
In our wake, light-bearing particles dance.

In our dreams
we cry out. Even if
it is merely the computer
brain sorting
recent days' info,
we do cry out, in our dreams:
some things
want to be heard, attended to,
hugged or killed,
known, before termination. Amen.
"Amen?" Yes,
that's an honest word.

Downstairs
they are improving themselves
by pounding bag.
That's it: pounding bag.

Upstairs
they are engaged in relentless
social as well as existential advance
toward the Great Dark
but not pretentious about it:
they "utilize,"
as they're apt to say,
a pretty good, simple program:

"Keep 'em stoned on the goods."

It may seem monotonous to some
(including us here on the middle floor,
decadents, no doubt,
easily amused, easily bored,
violent and lachrymose by turns:
not properly *grown*, I suppose)

but it certainly keeps the upstairs fellows
in some decent Scotch

Sonnet

There are many places in this world,
some of them inhabited by the totally mad.
She hands them pennies, directs them
to the nearest shelter.
Some we live right close to & somewhat
believe in, as further language.
Remember, too, the ones who died
while telling us they felt great
& the doctors agreed. The sun
shines upon the just & the wicked,
but why should they feel the same way
about how it feels, when no one hands them
a thermometer. As for thought,
I think it went out with Ted. He took
all the thought & sprinkled it all over
the globe, which is now clogging up
the toilet of this Star Wars universe.

"Go there!"   "Stay here!"
                "Stay there!"   "Come here!"
What changes
            is nothing but anywhere
they want you,
                and you want them to want you
there: and then
                there you are. Were.
Formerly there,
            now here. What do you know.
What a way to live. To have lived.
Nowhere. "One, very small,
                            to go."

Being chased out into the night
can be the beginning of a new life:

us human beings
ain't always benign,

but sometimes
            She is

And that's the difference between
"So be that way"
and "So be it."

*

How to join them,
the disparate, desperate "halves of the world"?

In the great sea smell of woman, of man,

                    of them together

*

Breathing, next to you
someone's telling you
you're not *all* there is –

"Surprise! Surprise!"
Laugh. Hurt
a little. Wonder

when it was you were
infinite, all-understanding
of, just, you.

*

84   Sunday: mission bells at six in the morning,
over thousands of small heavens and hells,
well, mostly purgatories. Give us a big kiss.

*

She changes. She does
what you did not expect her to do.
She'll always do that. It is
her way.

*

In places
there's a face
in place.

*

Saw her walking down the street one day

Remember grabbing ahold of small tree –

Midafternoon, sober, delighted, not knowing *what* to do
but to walk on.

*

Things
burn
off:

See
what's
left.

*

Sound of the summer's last cricket
haunting, that night, but all thoughts
of oblivion
banished
by your smile

as you moved close, and held, and whirred and pirouetted

your way into my soul, that rarely seen cousin
who lives in the house of memory

*

I love
your
back. I don't
have anywhere
to go back to
except for
your
back.

*

Time fills up, faster
and faster

But we
do
try to last

*

Sweet of you to say,
"Well, it'll give you a chance
to spend some time at your house,"
while knowing, as you must,
that any house I'm in where you are not

quite soon seems empty
until you walk in the door

*

This man who'd come down from the trees
had a lot of trouble with keys
but when he looked up again

he saw a tall woman
at the top of a stair
looking

and not looking one bit perturbed
by his frankly deplorable condition
(far past "mint")

and in her Greyte Kindnesse
she took him in
and even looked at his book

*

"What is love?" Well, we love
the sight of
                    the species
as it dances
                    at dusk

We would not want to miss it
for ever
            or ever

*

The faces
we make, making love,
are the only ones

will change our faces
over the years
into the ones we deserve

*

Insect-clock seasons pass, but the great pleasure
humans provide one another when so minded
is as close to perennial as creation gets

*

The dances of dusk are slow, because the dancers are.
Yet the dancers perceive them as fast,
excruciatingly fast,
and valiantly marshal their strength and cunning.

*

Voice, smile, hands moving

Hands moving, above all, most eloquently
in the rhetoric of making

Such a pleasure, to watch
the highly developed organism moving

and, as they say, doing

"Oh, doing it right"

*

Los gatos, eating their kind of food.
You, sleeping. Me, buzzed by
never-so-glad-ever: no more opera now but
some urgent intelligent weirdly impasssioned human life –

88   Never anywhere as this now: generosity: home: how is it
voluptas has become a word again?

    *

How was it when this world's people
thought things were *solid?*

In the light, they are

    *

The rich extended and exercised gentle paws.
The poor went to the scribe and said,
"Write: 'I miss you. Come soon.'"

And that was the beginning of poetry,
in Egypt.

Encouragement, From Two Hundred Years Ago

from the German of Reiner Kunze

At God's
feet, if God
has feet,

sitting
at his
feet, there's

       BACH—

not
the Magistrate of Leipzig

Composition in Joanna by Walker & Swenson, Book Typographers. Designed by Allan Kornblum. Coffee House Press books are printed on acid-free paper and are sewn in signatures to ensure durability.